ELT **Development Series**

SERIES EDITOR Thomas S. C. Farrell

REVISED EDITION

Teaching Pronunciation

John Murphy

tesolpress

tesol press
www.tesol.org/bookstore

TESOL International Association
1925 Ballenger Avenue
Alexandria, Virginia, 22314 USA
www.tesol.org

Director of Publishing and Product Development: Myrna Jacobs
Copy Editor: Meg Moss
Production Editor: Kari S. Dalton
Cover Design: Citrine Sky Design
Interior Design and Layout: Capitol Communications, LLC

ISBN 9781945351846
eBook ISBN 9781945351853
Library of Congress Control Number 2019956808

Table of Contents

Series Editor's Preface

The *English Language Teacher Development (ELTD)* series consists of a set of short resource books for ESL/EFL teachers that are written in a jargon-free and accessible manner for all types of teachers of English (native, nonnative, experienced, and novice). The ELTD series is designed to offer teachers a theory-to-practice approach to second language teaching, and each book presents a wide variety of practical approaches to and methods of teaching the topic at hand. Each book also offers reflections to help teachers interact with the materials presented. The books can be used in preservice settings or in in-service courses and by individuals looking for ways to refresh their practice. Now, after nearly 10 years in print, the ELTD series presents newly updated, revised editions that are even more dynamic than their first editions. Each of these revised books has an expanded number of chapters, as well as updated references from which various activities have been drawn and lesson plans for teachers to consider.

John Murphy's revised edition of *Teaching Pronunciation* again explores different approaches to teaching pronunciation in second language classrooms. John updated the references and research, and added more reflective questions as well as a detailed lesson plan that teachers can consider. This revised edition is again a valuable addition to the literature in our profession.

I am very grateful to the authors of the ELTD series for sharing their knowledge and expertise with other TESOL professionals to make these short books affordable for all language teachers throughout the world. It is truly an honor for me to work again with each of these authors for the advancement of TESOL.

Thomas S. C. Farrell

CHAPTER 1

Concepts to Support Teaching and Learning

To set the stage for a discussion of pronunciation teaching, look at the following excerpt adapted from a local television news report. In it, a female airline passenger is being interviewed about an emergency at the end of a long flight from Los Angeles to Miami. After introducing the woman as a "hero," the TV reporter asked her to describe her experiences on the plane. Please note that for reasons to be explained shortly, the transcript is intentionally punctuation-free.

The Airplane Aisle Incident

. . . the plane landed the cabin lights turned on everyone got out of their seats I stepped into the aisle opened the overhead compartment and was waiting my turn to leave the plane in back of me I heard a noise that didn't sound right when I turned I saw an older man was falling into a woman behind him he looked scared his face was stone white I didn't think he was breathing I yelled for help and then a couple of us moved into action the first thing I did was to get the people behind me to back away by this point most of the aisle had cleared so we were able to stretch him out on the floor I heard someone say we have to get him out of the plane so I grabbed his legs this tall guy grabbed his shoulders and we carried him off I know CPR so I cleared a space made sure everyone else was out of the way . . . fortunately when it was all over he fully recovered seemed to be fine . . .

Thought Groups and Pausing

A closer look at Excerpt 1 shows that the first few lines are divided into short segments based on the speaker's actual delivery:

The Airplane Aisle Incident: Excerpt 1

the plane landed // the cabin lights turned on // everyone got out of their seats // I stepped into the aisle // opened the overhead compartment // and was waiting my turn to leave the plane

---

The double slash marks indicate one of several rhythmic features that serve as momentary boundaries between clusters of words in spoken English. These may constitute a full break in the stream of speech, a lengthening, or a holding of the word at the end of a word cluster before the next cluster begins. Two examples of words that would be lengthened or held longer in this way are underlined:

> // the cabin lights turned **on** // everyone got out of their **seats** //

Lane (2010) explains that a lengthening or holding of syllables "may be heard as a pause, although within an utterance, the voice 'lingers' rather than stops" at the boundary of a word cluster (p. 52). For ease of presentation, I refer to such boundary markers as *pauses* and to the clusters of words between them as *thought groups*. Following these conventions, the double slash marks featured in Excerpt 1 indicate five pauses and six thought groups for what otherwise might have been an uninterrupted stream of speech. As the passenger related her story, her pauses were very brief, many barely noticeable, and most provided insufficient time for even a very quick intake of breath. Such pauses are a completely normal feature of spoken English that make possible its characteristic rhythmic nature (Brazil, 1994; Cauldwell, 2013; Levis, 2018). Pauses reflect momentary breaks in the flow of speech tied to the speaker's communicative intent as well as to both the speaker's and listener's needs for message organization. Though written texts in English provide clear divisions between words to simplify the process of reading, spoken English simply does not work that way. Rather, speakers speak in thought groups within which clusters of words are tightly strung together, thus forming intermittent pulses of speech (Lane, 2010; Murphy, 2017b).

Introducing Thought Groups

One way to introduce the concept of thought grouping to nonnative speakers of English is to present learners with examples of identical prepositions that sometimes occur together (Wong, 1987). More technically, these seemingly identical words usually involve the second element of a two-word verb followed immediately by the same word functioning as a preposition. Such dual occurrences of what appear to be the same words right next to each other can serve as powerful illustrations of the need for speakers to insert pauses at meaningful locations while speaking. Here are some examples:

- Why don't you think it over // over the weekend?
- What time does the doctor come in // in the afternoon?
- Who can we turn to // to learn more?
- This is exactly what I've been waiting for // for years.

Though this book covers additional facets of pronunciation as well, if the time available to teach pronunciation is limited, I suggest prioritizing the process of thought grouping. Or, if enough time to attend to other facets of pronunciation is available, be sure to teach the process of thought grouping early on and continue spiraling back to it. An awareness of how thought groups operate is essential for clearer understanding of most of the components of English pronunciation that are teachable in English as a second language (ESL) or English as a foreign language (EFL) classrooms (Brazil, 1994; Dickerson, 2010) because all such components are anchored within the thought group (Levis, 2018; Murphy, 2017b). Some priorities are to build learner awareness of what thought groups are, to define them in relation to the pauses that both straddle and help to delineate them, and to teach thought groups directly in language classrooms.

Why Are Thought Groups Helpful?

A compelling reason to teach the process of thought grouping is that it provides the time speakers need to organize their thoughts. Another reason is that when a speaker's message is well organized and presented in meaningful units, listeners have an easier time comprehending it (Reed, 2016). "The brief pauses or holding at the end of a thought group slows the student down [while speaking], giving him or her more time to make [appropriate] lexical, grammatical, and pronunciation choices" (Lane, 2010, p. 53). Here is a partial list of pronunciation features that may be taught more efficiently once learners are familiar with thought groups:

- prominence[1]
- stressed syllables within prominent words
- vowel peaks within stressed syllables
- consonants and consonant clusters
- naturally occurring phonological processes (e.g., deletion, linking, assimilation) that commonly occur across word boundaries but only within thought groups
- volume, pacing, and the rhythm of spoken English
- intonation

REFLECTIVE QUESTION

- What does the following imply with respect to pronunciation teaching?

Thought groups represent the phonological context for most of the more essential components of English pronunciation. If we ask what comes first—the prominent word, a stressed syllable, or any of the other bulleted items listed above—the answer is always the same. The thought group comes first.

---

[1] Sometimes called *focal stress*, *primary phrase stress*, and *sentence stress*.

A Familiar Illustration

Pauses and the pulses of thought groups between them serve as cues for listeners to more easily recognize grammatical units such as phrases and clauses within longer stretches of speech. Consider, for example, this familiar line from John F. Kennedy's 1961 U.S. presidential inaugural address:

> *Ask not what your country can do for you—*
> *ask what you can do for your country.*

As a quick YouTube search confirms, Kennedy divided this 17-word stretch into at least three, perhaps four, thought groups (parentheses indicate an optional or indistinct pause):

> // Ask not // what your country can do for you //
> ask what you (//) can do for your country //

Ask not—well, that's a thought group. Kennedy paused for a brief though perceptible moment both immediately before and after it. *Ask not* also happens to be a verb phrase and the stem of an imperative sentence. *What your country can do for you* is a noun clause that serves to complete the preceding verb phrase. Notice that each thought group corresponds with a coherent grammatical function even though it does not necessarily constitute a full sentence on its own. The pattern of using two thought groups to express a fuller idea repeats with the next phrase, *ask what you*, and its resolution, *can do for your country*. The speaker could have used fewer thought groups or even a single one for the entire set of 17 words; however, the impact on listeners might have been less memorable. As a seasoned politician aware of the persuasive power of language, President Kennedy was using the phenomenon of thought grouping to guide listeners for the purpose of maximum audience impact. Notice, too, that Kennedy projected some words within thought groups more forcefully than others. These more forcefully projected words are called *prominent* words. They may be represented as follows:

> // Ask **<u>not</u>** // what your country can do for **<u>you</u>** //
> ask what **<u>you</u>** (//) can do for your **<u>country</u>** //

I use bolding and underlining to call attention to the speaker's applications of prominence, a speech feature that corresponds with increased volume and vowel clarity. Notice that words made prominent in a speaker's delivery, and the characteristics of English pronunciation with which they correspond, all happen within the phonological context of the thought group.

How Do Thought Groups Work?

Speakers of English use pauses and the thought groups between them as tools for guiding listeners toward fuller understanding (Gilbert, 2009; Levis, 2018). Although no rigid rules dictate where the pauses straddling thought groups tend to appear, some general parameters are worth introducing in language classrooms. Pauses work best when they occur at locations that enhance meaningful communication (Murphy, 2016). Furthermore, the meaning the speaker is trying to convey is pivotal. Typically, pauses are not inserted between thought groups randomly; the system contains an internal logic (Reed, 2016). A central principle is that the insertion of pauses between thought groups depends on the speaker's pragmatic intent (the idea or effect the speaker is trying to convey; Cauldwell, 2013, 2018). To illustrate, consider Excerpt 2 from the Airplane Aisle Incident.

The Airplane Aisle Incident: Excerpt 2

opened the overhead compartment and was waiting my turn to leave the plane in back of me I heard a noise that didn't sound right when I turned I saw an older man was falling into a woman behind him

---

It would be very unlikely to insert pauses following the words *leave* and *me* because doing so would group the words *the plane in back of me* into a single thought group. Though an identically worded thought group might work perfectly well in a different context, here it would only confuse the listener (e.g., Was there another plane?). Because people's minds operate faster than their organs of speech, the speaker was already anticipating the

Teaching Pronunciation

subsequent sections of her narrative. By pausing momentarily after the word *plane* prior to saying *in back of me I heard a noise*, the speaker's pragmatic intent is made clear and a listener can more easily follow her story. Such subtle nuances in meaning are easier for listeners to recognize if the speaker is already providing relevant cues through the process of thought grouping.

As long as pause locations succeed in conveying the speaker's intended meaning, there is flexibility in the system. The process of thought grouping is sensitive to the dynamic, subtle, interpersonal contexts within which speakers and listeners interact (Brazil, 1994). Finally, speakers typically insert pauses to form thought groups comprising semantically and grammatically coherent word clusters (Celce-Murcia, Brinton, Goodwin, & Griner, 2010).

How Long Is a Thought Group?

Though a thought group can be as brief as a single word, listeners tend to perceive those of more than 7 to 9 words as rather long (Cauldwell, 2013, Murphy, 2017b). Anything more than about 10 to 12 words, though certainly possible, becomes increasingly problematic for listeners. Most of us are probably familiar with speakers of English whose sheer quantity of delivery as measured in number of words between pauses can sometimes overwhelm listeners. Though we may refer to such speakers as "fast talkers," the problematic feature of their speaking style is less a matter of the speed at which their organs of speech are moving and more likely a consequence of infrequent pauses within their streams of speech. Infrequent pausing results in longish, poorly delineated thought groups that listeners have trouble following and may perceive as uncomfortably rapid speech. The optimum size of a thought group (i.e., the number of words/syllables it contains) depends on intuitive decisions usually made beneath the level of a speaker's conscious attention. When necessary, however, speakers can take deliberate control of the process of thought grouping.

How Do Thought Groups Benefit Learners?

As language proficiency advances, a significant challenge learners face is to express themselves in longer speaking turns made up of consecutive thought groups (still separated by intermittent pauses) that are organized sensibly (Brown, 1977; Field, 2008). In fact, length of coherent speaking turn is one of the primary features differentiating levels of oral proficiency in English. Eventually, advanced ESL speakers reach a point when they can converse in interactive conversation through their use of multiple thought groups of related content during individual speaking turns (Brown, 1977). To help learners continue to move in this direction while also focusing on pronunciation, an appropriate teaching strategy is to build awareness of what thought groups are and how speakers can use them to be more clearly understood. As the earlier identical-prepositions activity illustrates, we can foster such awareness from the very earliest stages of language instruction (Miller & Jones, 2016). Here are some objectives for students:

- to become more mindful with respect to the process of thought grouping
- to fine-tune awareness until the process becomes second nature
- to develop intuition about when to let the process operate automatically and when to shift to more deliberate control

Definitions

Grant (2007) writes that "a thought group is a group of words that naturally go together" (p. 125). Celce-Murcia et al. (2010) define a thought group as a "discrete stretch of speech that forms a semantically and grammatically coherent segment of discourse" (p. 221).

REFLECTIVE QUESTION

- What does the following add to a working definition of thought groups?

  You should think of the [thought group] as the basic building block of spoken English. When language is written or printed, it appears to the eye as divided up into "words." When it is spoken it is heard by the ear as divided up into [thought groups]. Notice that the sounds that make up a [thought group] are usually run together in the way we are accustomed to thinking of the separate sounds of single words as being run together (modified from Brazil, 1994, p. 7).

Teaching Pronunciation

For learners who are ready for fuller discussion, we might add the following:

- A speaker creates a thought group; it is not formed automatically.
- Some speakers are better than others at thought grouping.
- Thought grouping is a central phonological process that English language learners can learn to work with effectively.
- A thought group corresponds with a rhythmic structure of speech that speakers can manipulate to good effect.
- If not a complete pause, a thought group's final stressed syllable is held before the next thought group begins (e.g., the single syllable in the word *seats* in the thought group: // everyone got out of their **seats** //).
- A thought group usually contains one particularly salient word (e.g., // in **back** of me //; // he fully **recovered** //).
- The thought group's most salient word will contain a primary stressed syllable on which the speaker's voice lingers. Furthermore, the vowel of this particular syllable will be more forcefully projected (louder) and will take a bit longer to enunciate than the vowels of the syllables around it (e.g., the vowel of *back* in the thought group // in **back** of me //; the vowel of the syllable *cov* in the thought group // he fully re**cov**ered //).
- Primary stressed syllables tend to coincide with the initiation of a distinct pitch movement (e.g., a slight drop or rise in pitch).

What Else Do Learners Need to Know?

Once such preliminary descriptions have been established, here are some related topics worth introducing to learners gradually over time:

- **Awareness**: A priority is to build awareness of the use of pauses to delineate thought groups.
- **Linking**: Words within a thought group are closely linked together (e.g., "What is the matter?" → "Smatter?"), whereas words across thought group boundaries do not link in this way.

- **Internal structure**: A thought group usually corresponds with a grammatical structure (Han, 2016; Rimmer, 2016) (e.g., a noun or verb phrase, a prepositional phrase, a relative clause).

- **Speaking rate**: Generally, a slower rate of speech leads to more, and more clearly delineated, thought groups.

- **Length**: Faster speech corresponds with fewer pauses and longer thought groups containing more words.

- **Intelligibility**: Because slower speech corresponds with more thought groups, listeners usually find speech that contains more frequent pauses and a higher number of recognizable thought groups easier to understand.

- **Limits to slower speech**: However, one's rate of speech can become excessively slow if there are just too many thought group divisions (Derwing & Munro, 2015). Goodwin (2001) explains that a common error of "less fluent speakers is pausing too frequently, thereby overloading the listener with too many breaks to process the discourse effectively" (p. 119).

- **Goldilocks principle:** An appropriate long-term strategy is to develop a moderate rate of speech (i.e., not too fast [too few thought groups] and not too slow [too many thought groups]) to be optimally intelligible (Derwing & Munro, 2015; Levis, 2018).

- **Register**: More formal registers of speech tend to correspond with more frequent pauses and a correspondingly larger number of thought groups containing fewer words (e.g., political speech).

- **Time to monitor**: Pauses provide ESL/EFL speakers with more time to self-monitor and make appropriate choices while speaking.

REFLECTIVE QUESTIONS

- In your own words, how would you define *thought groups* for a class of ESL/EFL learners?

- What resources might you use to illustrate the process of thought grouping?

- How would you respond to a skeptical learner who asks, "Why are we learning about thought groups?"

Conclusion

The purpose of developing a moderate speaking rate with a relevant degree of thought grouping is so that listeners can more easily understand ESL/EFL speakers. A teacher's challenge is to provide opportunities for learners to incorporate an appropriate degree of pausing in their speech, at locations that make sense, so that learners' speech consists of thought groups their listeners will perceive as containing reasonable numbers of words. Given the general benefits associated with a moderate rate of speech, it is profitable for teachers to guide students in the use of thought groups for more effective communication. Ideally, they will learn to adjust their speaking rates to best fit the communicative situation. To do so, pronunciation instruction should prioritize opportunities to learn about the process of thought grouping at all levels of proficiency (i.e., beginning through advanced) via awareness raising, direct instruction, and plenty of practice opportunities.

The chapters to follow offer a practical model for teaching pronunciation reflecting these initial priorities. The model's purposes are to illustrate instructional possibilities grounded in contemporary theory (e.g., Cauldwell, 2013, 2018; Derwing & Munro, 2015; Dickerson, 2010; Levis, 2018) and teaching practice (e.g., Gilbert, 2009; Grant, 2017; Jones, 2016; Murphy, 2017c) and to serve as a starting point from which teachers may modify some of the ideas offered to best fit their learners' needs. Chapter 2 focuses on preplanning tasks teachers need to complete prior to classroom teaching. Chapters 3 through 5 discuss six other important facets of pronunciation worth teaching once learners are aware of and have begun to work with the process of thought grouping. These facets are prominence, featured words, rehearsal strategies, syllables, word stress, and the vowel system.

What Teachers Need to Do

To prepare to teach pronunciation, a teacher's first task is to locate a good selection of language samples that will be appropriate for the proficiency level of the class (Murphy, 2016). Though a combination of both written and oral language samples is recommended, I focus on ways of working with written samples because written texts serve as centerpieces for ESL/EFL teaching in most classrooms worldwide. If the course already focuses on pronunciation, the students' textbook likely contains plenty of useful language samples. Many teachers, however, want to be able to pay at least some attention to pronunciation in courses that are not pronunciation focused. Some very good news is that even in more broadly focused courses, potentially useful language samples abound.

An appropriate language sample for teaching pronunciation may be as uncomplicated as an introductory dialogue from a beginning-level text or as challenging as a transcript of an academic lecture from an advanced-level listening for academic purposes text. All such materials can be useful, depending on the characteristics of the language sample and the learners' level of proficiency. We should also think about the length, in number of words, of a potential language sample. For courses geared toward lower proficiency levels, texts between 50 and 170 words are probably long enough. This would be the typical length of dialogues and paragraphs featured in lower-level EFL classroom textbooks. The Airplane Aisle Incident narrative presented in chapter 1 is just under 190 words and suggests that texts between 170 and 250 words would suffice for intermediate-level classes. Students at high-intermediate and advanced levels of proficiency may work with language samples that are considerably longer. Higher-level courses may also begin to incorporate a mix of written texts accompanied by audio recordings (e.g., transcripts of interviews that feature first language and other advanced-level speakers of English, podcasts, radio broadcasts, lectures). Here are some steps to follow prior to pronunciation teaching:

- Find language samples of appropriate length that meet learners' needs.
- Include samples of written language featuring at least some characteristics of spoken discourse.
- Consider both commercially published and self-generated language samples.
- Include source materials from different media (e.g., books, internet, radio, TV).
- Prioritize language samples appearing in the class textbook already featured in the course.

In addition to written texts, samples of spoken language generated live in the classroom may also be used. Approaches to language teaching, such as the Direct Method, Language Experience Approach, and Community Language Learning, describe procedures for transcribing samples of spoken language generated live in the classroom (Brown & Lee, 2015). More conventionally, most ESL and EFL textbooks, even those designed to teach integrated skills, reading, writing, or grammar, include either scripted simulations of speech or prose selections that can be very effective as supports for pronunciation teaching. Segments of audio podcasts such as National Public Radio's *Fresh Air* and *StoryCorps* are appropriate if the content has been screened for suitability. Alternatively, it is a good idea to sometimes use language samples you generate on your own (e.g., the Airplane Aisle Incident). In sum, the first step in preparing to teach pronunciation is to locate a sufficient number of language samples (e.g., one or more per week) that are relevant to students' level of proficiency, of appropriate length, and interesting enough to both capture and maintain student interest.

REFLECTIVE QUESTIONS

- Which of the following do you think are more useful to include as core language samples: dialogues, monologues, narratives; scripted, semiscripted, or authentic language samples; excerpts from lectures, podcasts, textbooks, screenplays, novels, TV interviews, radio shows, film screenplays, corpus resources, EAP listening materials?

- What criteria would you apply when selecting text types to use in class?

- In an ESL/EFL textbook you are currently using, locate two to three sections that provide potentially useful language samples. What characteristics are you considering?

Preparing Language Samples

Once you have identified an appropriate language sample, you need to decide if it will be more helpful to employ as either a *general* or a *core* language sample. General language samples can be used as they are. Typically, these are brief sections from students' textbooks that may serve to introduce, illustrate, and reinforce the concept of thought grouping or other pronunciation features. In contrast, core samples require more preparation because they will serve as centerpieces for instruction. A large concern is that core language samples need to be reformatted ahead of time. As with the Airplane Aisle Incident narrative, the idea is to reformat core samples to remove nearly all of their punctuation (Murphy 2015, 2016). In most instances, this means retyping them and saving them as newly reformatted electronic files. It is especially important to retype and reformat language samples from a textbook, otherwise the removal of punctuation is impossible. Because students will be marking such materials up extensively, double-spacing is recommended. The remainder of this book prioritizes core language samples in pronunciation teaching. It is worth keeping in mind, however, that general samples from students' textbooks sometimes are useful. In sum, once core language samples have been identified, the teacher needs to retype them to present to learners in a format that is nearly punctuation-free.[2]

Introducing the Language Sample in Class

Once a core language sample is in place, the next question is: How will I present it to the class? Sometimes a combination of audio and written versions is needed. For teachers interested in exposing learners to different voices of English speakers, audio recordings and YouTube displays may be used. For most activities, a written version is required because students will at times be analyzing it closely for subsequent work on pronunciation. Some possibilities for presenting language samples include

- Everyone gets a photocopy (preferred).
- A copy is displayed at the front of the room (e.g., poster paper, PowerPoint).
- Students create their own written version through teacher-fronted listening dictation or dicto-comp activities.[3]
- Other classroom procedures such as information gaps, jigsaw procedures, strip sentences, and cloze exercises may also be used.

---

[2] Although the term "punctuation-free" is featured throughout this discussion, both capitalization of the personal pronoun "I" and the inclusion of apostrophes to signal (a) possession and (b) contractions need to be maintained when using otherwise "punctuation-free" samples of written language.

[3] Dicto-comp is a technique in which the teacher reads a language sample aloud and students write out what they understand and remember while trying to keep as close as possible to the original.

Conclusion

This chapter focused on tasks a classroom teacher needs to complete ahead of time to prepare for pronunciation teaching. The tasks are to (1) locate language samples relevant to learners' needs, (2) create written versions that are punctuation-free, and (3) decide how to present them in class. These preparatory steps are necessary so that students will be able to work closely with useful samples of English as a basis for pronunciation work. The best appropriate language samples are either authentic samples of spoken language for which a written e-transcript is readily available (e.g., TEDTalks; the Santa Barbara Corpus of Spoken American English) or written texts that reflect at least some of the characteristics of spoken English. The next chapter explains how to guide students in the productive use of such core language samples, and it features a lesson plan that illustrates recommended classroom procedures.

CHAPTER 3

What Students Need to Do

This chapter discusses the primary tasks students will be asked to complete as a necessary foundation for work on pronunciation. As outlined in chapter 1, thought groups constitute the phonological environment within which most essential features of pronunciation happen. By beginning with the process of thought grouping, teachers can then use it as an anchor for subsequent stages of teaching pronunciation. Lane (2010) suggests that both teachers and students find the process of thought grouping to be a particularly accessible pronunciation feature, one that can be taught success-fully in many kinds of ESL/EFL classrooms. Specialists such as Brazil (1994), Cauldwell (2013, 2018), Dickerson (2010), and Murphy (2017c) recommend that the process of thought grouping needs to be the starting point if later pronunciation topics are going to make sense to learners.

Learning Objectives

The first objective is for learners to be able to identify thought groups within the core language sample presented to them. To prepare students, the teacher needs to (1) define and teach what thought groups are, (2) provide illustrations, (3) demonstrate how and why speakers use thought groups, (4) explain and illustrate strategies for locating thought groups in punctuation-free written texts, (5) provide a printed language sample so that students' work can begin, and (6) show learners how to insert slash marks to signal pauses between thought groups.

Once this preparatory work is completed and students have access to a punctuation-free language sample, the teacher asks them to locate as many thought groups as seems sensible within the sample provided (see Lesson Plan #1). Pair or small-group work is useful at this stage. To keep track of the thought groups they identify, students should use an erasable pencil or pen to mark boundaries between thought groups, as illustrated in chapter 1. While students are engaged in this task, teachers should be prepared to respond to their many questions. Once students have found a reasonable number of thought groups, they may move on to rehearsing the language sample aloud in pairs. Their charge is to practice saying at least a dozen of the thought groups aloud several times each while learning to insert pauses between them.

An Application Task

Here is an example of the learning tasks just described. Your challenge is to try to figure out what the speaker's thought groups might have been while attending to some of the nuances in meaning the speaker was likely intending to convey.

Identifying Thought Groups in the Airplane Aisle Incident[4]

Directions: Insert double slash marks to indicate likely pause locations in the speaker's stream of speech.

Example:

the plane landed // the cabin lights turned on // everyone got out of their seats // I stepped into the aisle // opened the overhead compartment // and was waiting my turn to leave the plane //

- In back of me I heard a noise that didn't sound right when I turned I saw an older man was falling into a woman behind him

- He looked scared his face was stone white I didn't think he was breathing

- I yelled for help and then a couple of us moved into action the first thing I did was to get the people behind me to back away by this point most of the aisle had cleared

- so we were able to stretch him out on the floor I heard someone say we have to get him out of the plane so I grabbed his legs this tall guy grabbed his shoulders and we carried him off I know CPR so I cleared a space made sure everyone else was out of the way

- fortunately when it was all over he fully recovered seemed to be fine

The task you have just completed illustrates one of the most important tools for effective communication in English, the process of thought grouping. This brief illustration is intended to serve as a prototype for designing, building upon, and further developing your own classroom activities.

REFLECTIVE QUESTIONS

- What difficulties did you have in completing the thought group identification task?

- What additional difficulties do you anticipate students might have?

- How might you introduce the task of *rehearsing the language sample aloud* to a group of language learners?

- How might you modify such a task to better suit students' needs?

---

[4] See the Appendix for answer key related to this and later application tasks.

Prominence

Once learners are comfortable working with thought groups, the second feature of pronunciation to teach is *prominence*. Notice that discussions of prominence are meaningless until an appreciation for thought grouping has first been established. Although an awareness of thought grouping helps delineate the landscape for pronunciation work, prominence is the anchor of the rhythm system of spoken English (Cauldwell, 2013; Hahn, 2004; Field, 2008). To focus on prominence, a useful task is to ask students to identify prominent words in the thought groups with which they have already been working. What they need to know is that some words within a thought group, and always at least one word, stand out in relation to the other words surrounding them. Consider the word in bold print for each of the following thought groups:

// sorry to **bother** you //

// don't **mention** it //

// this is **fantastic** news //

Prominence refers to the tendency in spoken English for one word within a thought group to stand out in a listener's perceptual field (Sardegna, Chiang, & Ghosh, 2016). It is the word that a speaker "punches out" more forcefully (i.e., with more acoustic energy) relative to its neighboring words. The construct of prominence is relational because it refers to a relative degree of acoustic salience among the words of the thought group being considered (Hahn, 2004; Murphy, 2017b). That is, a prominent word is a bit louder within the thought group and therefore will be more noticeable. Another important point to teach is that within a prominent word of more than one syllable, the word's primary stressed syllable specifically bears the prominence feature most (e.g., the first syllable of *bother*, the first syllable of *mention*, the second syllable of *fantastic* in the preceding examples). Again, the construct of prominence is relational because not all syllables are treated equally even at the level of an individual word (Cauldwell, 2013). The primary stressed vowel of a prominent word within a thought group is not only louder, it also takes a bit longer to enunciate. As Goodwin (2001) explains, "within each thought group, there is generally one *prominent* element, a particular syllable [within a prominent word] that is emphasized" (p. 119). This happens because the speaker's voice lingers a bit longer on the peak vowel of a prominent word's primary stressed syllable (Lane, 2010).

REFLECTIVE QUESTION

- In the following dialogue, why does Justin's use of the word *you* receive prominence whereas David's initial use of the same word does not? Also, why is *hated* a prominent word in Justin's final speaking turn?

David: *Hey! Good to <u>see</u> you. How <u>are</u> you?*

Justin: *I'm doing well. How are <u>you</u>?*

David: *Everything's good. I saw Pat yesterday. She said you just got back from a cruise.*

Justin: *Oh, don't remind me. I <u>hated</u> it. Too much food, too many people, and the cabins were tiny. If you ever go on cruise, make sure you have a good book.*

In general, speakers use prominent words as navigational cues for directing (and refocusing) conversations while the trajectory of the conversation is still unfolding (Gilbert, 2009; Sardegna et al., 2016). Prominence is highly sensitive to contextual considerations and a speaker's pragmatic intent. For this reason, it is not useful for English language learners to examine or discuss prominence in sentences or thought groups presented out of context, a pervasive and persistent problem with many ESL/EFL textbooks (Levis, 1999, 2018). Better understanding of how prominence operates also allows speakers to spice up what they have to say. When Justin used *hated* as a prominent word in the example above, its introduction was unexpected, and the tone of the conversation shifted as a result.

To prepare students to work with prominence, a teacher must do four things:

- Define and teach what prominence is.
- Provide plenty of contextualized illustrations.
- Demonstrate how and why speakers use prominence within thought groups.
- Explain and illustrate strategies for locating prominent words.

Once students seem ready, they can begin to build upon their work with the same language sample they have already divided into thought groups. Their new task is to locate at least one prominent word for each of the sample's thought groups. A straightforward way to set prominent words apart is to circle (or underline) them. Periodically, student pairs or small groups can discuss and compare their efforts.

REFLECTIVE QUESTIONS

- Return to your work earlier in this chapter on the identification of thought groups in the Airplane Aisle Incident narrative. This time, circle at least one prominent word for each of the thought groups you identified. (The Appendix provides an answer key.)

- Consider alternative ways of introducing the concept of prominence to a group of language learners. What resources might you use? How would you explain the concept so that students can easily understand?

After prominent words have been identified, rehearsing the language sample aloud can resume. This time, students can begin to focus on their use of prominence within thought groups. Their new challenge will be to employ increased volume and vowel lengthening while rehearsing as complementary signals of prominence.

For students who are ready for a slightly fuller explanation, you can discuss the special role played by the primary stressed syllable of prominent words. Such a syllable is not only a bit louder and lasts longer than other syllables, it also coincides with a perceptible change in tone (Levis, 2018). Tone shifts in English (either a slight rise or a slight fall of a speaker's voice) begin on the vowel of the prominent word's most strongly stressed syllable (Levis, 1999; Sardegna et al., 2016). To review: the three pronunciation features used to express prominence are (1) increased volume, (2) a lengthening of the prominent word's primary stressed syllable, and (3) a tone shift either up or down on the stressed syllable.

Featured Words

After students have worked with thought groups and prominence in the first two sets of pronunciation tasks, they may begin to notice that some thought groups contain more than just a single salient word. At this point (and especially when learners begin to ask about it), you can explain that if multiple words receive special attention (i.e., stress) within a thought group, English speakers tend to pronounce one of the words a bit more forcefully than any others. As discussed earlier, the word most forcefully pronounced is the prominent word; other more lightly stressed words may be referred to as *featured* words. Here is an example:

// I like buying used cars **<u>too</u>** //

In this thought group, prominence falls on the word *too*, whereas *I* is a less strongly stressed "featured" word. Discussing featured words provides opportunities to both reinforce and more fully define how prominent words operate within thought groups. Furthermore, it presents opportunities to explore how such salient words function in relation to each other within the phonological context of the broader language sample. By examining the pronunciation features of thought grouping, prominence, and featured words in relation to each other, students are more likely to understand more clearly the respective roles each plays in English pronunciation.

Here is another example:

// there are literally **hundreds** of <u>cities</u> that we could have <u>visited</u> //

In this 11-word example, *hundreds* is the prominent word because it is most heavily laden with new information, but both *cities* and *visited* also receive some degree of stress. Though one could argue that *literally* might also carry stress, it is more likely that *literally* would remain unstressed to leave plenty of acoustic space for prominence to be placed on the word immediately following it. In contrast to the pronunciation systems of many other languages, such relative degrees of either backgrounding or foregrounding neighboring words is one of the fundamental rhythmic features of English (Cauldwell, 2013; Levis, 2018). For teaching purposes, we can refer to words such as *cities* and *visited* as featured words, whereas prominence is reserved for *hundreds* in this example. Rules for which word is most prominent in relation to the others depend on the speaker's pragmatic intent. A full context of communication needs to be available for a speaker's meaning to become apparent.

Teachers need to realize that speakers use similar phonological qualities to signal both featured words and prominent words. These qualities are volume (they are produced more loudly) and time (they take longer to say). In the case of prominent words, there may also be a slight rise or a slight fall in the speaker's voice, initiated at the word's primary stressed syllable. These qualities tend to fall on content-laden words determined not by grammatical category or some implicit characteristic of stress-timing in English, but, even more essentially, by the meaning focus of the speaker's conversational flow (Cauldwell, 2013, 2018). Also, a simple guideline is that featured words outnumber prominent words in English speech.

Along with the phenomenon of primary stressed syllables, an intonation change within a thought group normally initiates on the primary stressed syllable of a prominent word; see the underlined syllables in this example:

// and it would **rea**lly be a disaster (//) if my **step**father showed up //

Furthermore, new information tends to be featured prominently, and old information does not. Imagine that the following two thought groups are spoken in sequence by the same person:

1. // I can think of **three** of her **cousins** who I'd **really** like to **invite** to the **wedding** //

2. // and I can think of **three** of **my** cousins who I really **don't** want to invite at **all** //

Notice that item 1 features the word *cousins*, but for item 2, a listener would already realize that *cousins* are part of the topic of conversation; therefore the same word no longer needs to be foregrounded within the stream of speech. As shared information previously established, *cousins* may now recede to the background of the conversation. For items 3 through 5 appearing in the following Reflective Question, consider how a series of prominent words would emerge in reference to other family members if the same speaker were to continue voicing his or her concerns.

REFLECTIVE QUESTIONS

For items 3 through 5, see if you can figure out which five words (only) would likely be the prominent words. When you locate them, circle each one:

3. // but I want my sisters to be there // no matter what //

4. // I hope my father stays away //

5. // it would really be a disaster (//) if my stepfather showed up //

Now, provide some justification for why the five words you selected would be prominent. Are there any other words that might be featured but not prominent?

In item 5, *stepfather* is prominent as a result of the speaker wanting to contrast it with the use of *father* in item 4. Generally, words used in contrast to something previously mentioned tend to serve as prominent words. We can simultaneously define and illustrate this principle of *contrastive stress* in the following by imagining that a single speaker is contrasting the words *new* and *old*:

// **new** information tends to be made **prominent**//

// while **old** information does **not** //

Finally, words used emphatically also tend to be prominent, such as *don't* and *all* in this illustration from item 2 above:

// who I really **don't** want to invite at **all** //

Similar emphatic stress is used on the word *really* in item 5. Although this is not an exhaustive list of phonological conditions that lead to prominent and featured words, it is more than enough to guide students in their analyses of most language samples.

Recapping the Learning Tasks So Far

By now, students have spent considerable time with a core language sample and have come to know it well. They have identified its thought groups, prominent elements, and featured words. Eventually, students should discuss the content of the selection more extemporaneously, as well as any other elements of pronunciation they are noticing. In addition, teachers will need to complement the types of rehearsal activities emphasized here with more fluency-building activities such as discussions, games, role-plays, mock interviews, simulations, and so forth. By calling attention to a manageable number of core pronunciation features, however, teachers can better prepare learners to apply such features when speaking extemporaneously. It is up to the teacher to decide how long students will continue to work with the same language sample (perhaps in consultation with the class) or when it might be time to introduce a different one and begin the process again. For simplicity of presentation throughout the remainder of the book, I assume that subsequent stages will continue to use the same language sample.

REFLECTIVE QUESTIONS

- What are some advantages of continuing to work with a single language sample over the span of several classes? Some disadvantages?

- What criteria would you apply for deciding when to move students on to a new language sample?

- Can you list any advantages of sometimes consulting students while making such teaching decisions?

Rehearsal

Rehearsal procedures represent a culmination of students' work on pronunciation so far. These are opportunities to consolidate knowledge and to grow more comfortable with the pronunciation features being introduced. When rehearsing, students' tasks are to (a) practice the language sample aloud while applying what they have learned, (b) delineate thought groups with pauses, and (c) modulate their voices to signal both prominent and featured words.

Across all proficiency levels, the Read-Look-Up-and-Say (RLUS) procedure can serve as a starting point for student peer-to-peer rehearsals (see Fanselow, 1987). RLUS is similar to how a professional actor works with an acting coach one-on-one, face-to-face, with scripts in hand. As a way of introducing RLUS, the teacher might lead a discussion of how and why actors prepare for performances by rehearsing written scripts aloud. Morley (1994) recommends RLUS variations such as strong vigorous practice, exaggerated practice, self-monitoring, slow-motion and half-speed practice, loop ("broken record") practice, whispering practice, as well as the use of mirrors and video while rehearsing (p. 86). Audio and video functions featured on smartphones and tablets are particularly useful to enable either self-viewing (live) or self-recording. Audio and video recordings make it possible for students to analyze their speaking efforts closely, either individually or with classmates.

REFLECTIVE QUESTIONS

● What difficulties might students have with peer-to-peer rehearsal procedures?

● What are some advantages (and disadvantages) of having students audio-record or video-record themselves during such rehearsals?

● What learning tasks would you design for students listening to or reviewing recordings of their own speech?

● How might the incorporation of other technology and internet-mediated forms of language instruction enhance the teaching procedures discussed in this chapter?

Conclusion

This chapter introduced the central learning tasks featured in the book. The procedures included the use of a core language sample as a basis for pronunciation work as well as several tasks that ask students to identify thought groups, prominent words, and featured words. The final section illustrated some options for getting learners to rehearse a core language sample aloud, in ways similar to how actors prepare for public performances. By placing the process of thought grouping, prominent words, and featured words at the center of pronunciation teaching, teachers give students opportunities to focus their energies in a direction that will really make a difference in the quality of their speech (Cauldwell, 2013) and the degree to which listeners will understand them (Hahn, 2004). By doing so, teachers structure the limited time available for pronunciation teaching on pivotal rather than peripheral concerns (Dickerson, 2010; Levis, 2018). Lesson Plan #1 centers on these procedures.

Lesson Plan #1
Teaching the Process of Thought Grouping

Level: Low-Intermediate	**Time:** 30–45 minutes
Source: Murphy, J. (2015, 2016)	
Learning Objectives: Students will identify thought groups while reading along with and listening to a 190-word recorded audio broadcast.	
Language Focus: The process of thought grouping, word clusters	
Anticipated Problems: Because students are not used to working with punctuation-free language samples, they may be confused when first asked to do so. Students may not realize some of the important differences between the conventions of written and spoken texts.	
Solutions: Explain what a punctuation-free language sample is and why it can be a useful tool for learning about the process of thought grouping. Show the class a few examples of what a punctuation-free text looks like. Be clear that the activity focuses on characteristics of spoken language. Point out a few of the distinctions between written and spoken texts (e.g., printed texts consistently show blank spaces between individual words but in spoken texts, clusters of words tend to be squished together and have far fewer acoustic spaces between them).	
Materials: Find an audio (or audio plus video) recording from TV, radio, the internet, or some other media source that presents a narrative that would be assessible to students after a second or third listening. An example suitable for a low-intermediate class is the Airplane Aisle Incident featured in chapter 1. Ahead of time, transcribe (or copy-paste if an e-transcription is available) the full narrative using a word processor. While typing it up, remove most of its punctuation including all commas, semicolons, periods, sentence breaks, paragraph breaks, and so on. Also remove any extra spaces between sentences, and do not capitalize the first words of sentences. However, you will need to keep instances of the personal pronoun "I" as a capital letter, the capitalization of any proper nouns, and conventional spaces between individual words. Maintain apostrophes used for contractions and possessives as well. Once the nearly punctuation-free narrative is ready, double-space it, insert line numbers for every other line, and print out enough copies for students in the class. Finally, make sure each student has a pencil with an eraser.	

continued on next page

Teaching Pronunciation

Classroom Procedures

1. Explain that students will be working with a punctuation-free written transcription of an audio text (e.g., a narrative) to learn more about the process of thought grouping.

2. Briefly define and illustrate what thought groups are while using a few examples from materials previously covered in the course.

3. Explain that proficient speakers of English speak in thought groups. These may be defined as clusters of words in connected speech that speakers normally link together. Also explain that thought groups are normally straddled by brief pauses and thereby constitute pulses of speech.

4. Make the point that most of the listeners they meet will find those who use thought groups well easier to understand.

5. Divide the class into groups of two and give each student a copy of the punctuation-free narrative.

6. Play the recorded audio/video narrative once (more if needed) and review its content with the class. Address students' questions about its content and requests for clarification as needed. Leave a few minutes for discussion.

7. Explain that as they listen to the recording once more, their task is to use a pencil to insert slanted lines (e.g., //) at the end of each thought group they hear.

8. Remind the class that although the printed text includes no punctuation clues, thought groups tend to coincide with meaningful grammatical units (e.g., noun clauses, verb clauses) and that brief pauses usually straddle them. Also, ask students to attend closely to other qualities of the speaker's voice (tone shifts, lingering on certain words), as these may also signal thought group boundaries.

9. Model the procedure (e.g., via whiteboard, Power Point, SmartBoard).

10. Depending upon the level of the class, provide one or more opportunities for students to listen to the recording as they identify the speaker's thought groups on their own.

11. Eventually, ask pairs of students to compare their work and build toward whole-class discussion of thought group phenomena (e.g., definitions, characteristics, illustrations, frequency, length, variations in use, impacts of intelligibility).

12. To shift to a production focus, have pairs of students practice aloud some of the thought groups they have identified.

13. For more spontaneous speech, lead students in a review and discussion of the narrative's content, any questions its content may have raised as well as any features they notice about the process of thought grouping.

14. Eventually, students can be guided as they continue to rehearse the language sample aloud, further analyze it, and/or discuss its content more extemporaneously.

15. For students at either a lower or higher level of English proficiency, select an alternative language sample that is either easier or more challenging to understand.

continued on next page

Other Options

1. The lesson plan presented above depicts a "listen-to-the-recording-first" procedure. A different option would ask students to work with the written version of the (punctuation-free) narrative before they have any opportunity to listen to it. In this way, students can be asked to make their best guesses concerning the locations of pauses between thought groups before listening to the recording. Again, students can first work alone and then compare what they have come up with in pairs, small groups, or with the whole class. Later, they can listen to the recording to compare what they anticipated would be the narrator's thought groups with the recorded evidence of the speaker's actual delivery. Students are often surprised by some of the differences between what they thought they would hear and the thought groups a speaker actually uses.

2. For more advanced students, audio narratives selected for the course could come from popular sources such as TedTalks, The Education Portal, and National Public Radio (e.g., *Fresh Air, Hidden Brain*). These and similar sources make e-transcripts of their audio/video broadcasts easily available on the internet. Once you have generated and distributed a punctuation-free version of an excerpt of such a recording, students can use their own smartphones to work with the paired audio and written materials both in the classroom and at home. Eventually, students can begin to search for, self-select, and send to their instructor internet links to podcasts they would like to use in class.

Syllable Counts and Word Stress

Chapters 1–3 established a landscape for pronunciation teaching. They focused on the process of thought grouping, a topic that embraces the roles of prominence and featured words in the pronunciation of English. Building upon these relatively broad components, chapter 4 will describe how characteristics of individual words interact with thought groups and prominence. These characteristics include a prominent word's total number of syllables, the location of its primary stressed syllable, and patterns of word stress. Just as discussions of prominence are meaningless until appreciation for the process of thought grouping has been established, the characteristics of individual words discussed in this chapter are better appreciated once the construct of prominence has been introduced.

Number of Syllables Within a Word

To know how to pronounce a word clearly in English, the speaker needs to get its number of syllables right (Cutler, 2015). One reason is that listeners anticipate hearing the right number of syllables arranged in a particular pattern of word-level stress (Field, 2005, 2008).[5] Another reason is that getting the number of syllables right lays a necessary foundation for the speaker to be able to (1) stress the word's primary syllable, (2) produce the vowel sound of that particular syllable with at least a threshold level of precision, and (3) leave the word's remaining syllables unstressed or only lightly stressed, as appropriate. For example, the unusually long word *overgeneralization* contains eight syllables. Its primary stressed syllable is the seventh, and that is the syllable English language listeners expect to hear most clearly.

						/	
o	ver	gen	er	al	i	za	tion
1	2	3	4	5	6	7	8

As previewed in chapter 3, being able to figure out a word's syllable count is especially important for prominent words because listeners depend most upon them. To foster such awareness, the teacher needs to define what syllables are, provide examples, and illustrate that each syllable of an English word usually contains one vowel. Although these are relatively easy ideas for students to understand conceptually, it takes focused practice before such understanding begins to make a difference in pronunciation. As the next step in working with a core language sample, teachers ask students to focus on the prominent words they have already identified (see chapter 3) while figuring out the number of syllables for at least a handful of them.

REFLECTIVE QUESTIONS

- What are some tips and strategies you would share with students for learning to identify the number of syllables in a word? Might any hand gestures be involved? Dictionary work? The use of smartphones?

---

[5] Relationships between syllable counts, pronunciation, and a listener's perception of words are more complex than space limitations permit discussion of here. Cauldwell (2013, 2018), for example, documents that fast-fluent speakers of English often suppress some syllables and may shift prominence and primary word stress locations within thought groups.

Teaching Pronunciation

Celce-Murcia et al. (2010), Grant (2017), and Lane (2010) provide many classroom activities designed to focus learners' attention on discerning the number of syllables in English words. When working with such resources in conjunction with core language samples, I ask students to create a list of prominent words and to label each word with its number of syllables (see Murphy, 2004, 2014). During subsequent rehearsal activities, students practice saying prominent words aloud while focusing on getting their number of syllables right.

Primary Stressed Syllables

Along with identifying the number of syllables in a word, an equally important step is to locate the word's primary stressed syllable. As before, priority should be given to prominent words within thought groups. In preparation, the teacher might consult resources such as Dauer (1993, pp. 67–69), Celce-Murcia et al. (2010, pp. 187–194), and the many easy-to-find internet resources that offer accessible rules for determining primary stressed syllables. To cite two examples, the primary stressed syllable for words ending in the suffixes –tion, –sion, –ic, –ical, –ity, and –graphy is almost always the syllable immediately before the suffix (e.g., elec*tri*city, edu*ca*tion). Also, two-syllable words such as *permit* and *conduct*, which can function as either nouns or verbs, usually carry primary stress on their first syllable when functioning as nouns and on their second syllable when functioning as verbs.

REFLECTIVE QUESTIONS

- What are some other rules for identifying a prominent word's primary stressed syllable?

- Why might learners find coverage of such rules to be helpful?

- Where would you look to learn more about this feature of pronunciation?

To introduce the topic, teachers need to define what primary stressed syllables are while demonstrating that such syllables sound a bit louder and take a bit longer to pronounce. Such discussion provides opportunities to make connections with several of the concepts featured in chapter 3. Just as both prominent words and featured words may appear within a single thought group, both primary stressed and secondary stressed syllables may occur within a single word. Revisiting our earlier example, the word *overgeneralization* receives primary stress on its seventh syllable, while both its first and third syllables receive some degree of secondary stress.

\		\				/	
o	ver	**gen**	er	al	i	**za**	tion
1	2	3	4	5	6	7	8

REFLECTIVE QUESTION

● How might you explain the following analogies to students? What concepts are they intended to convey?

   a. *Prominent words are to thought groups as primary stressed syllables are to individual words.*

   b. *Prominent words are to featured words as primary stressed syllables are to secondary stressed syllables.*

Students need to realize listeners can more easily understand speakers who consistently get primary stressed syllables right (Cutler, 2015; Field, 2005, 2008). When students are ready, their next task in working with a core language sample is to insert a superscript accent mark (′) directly above the primary stressed syllable (e.g., móther) for each of the prominent words they identify. Working in pairs or small groups, learners can compare their efforts and continue rehearsing the language sample aloud while focusing on primary stressed syllables. To make these prominent syllables clear, students should be applying the pronunciation features of increased volume and vowel lengthening.

Word Stress Patterns

Once learners begin to see that primary stressed syllables distinguish the prominent words within thought groups, everyone in the classroom needs an easy and straightforward way to talk about primary stressed syllables. This stage is important because it will be easier to notice, talk about, and remember word stress patterns if everyone shares conventions for discussing them (Murphy, 2004). By this point in the learning process, students have already identified the number of syllables in each prominent word and they have located the words' primary stressed syllables. We can now teach an easy-to-remember labeling system for identifying word stress patterns. To accomplish this, I introduce a simple two-digit numbering system (see Murphy, 2014; Murphy & Kandil, 2004). For example, the word *communication* is a 5-4 word. This means that *communication* is a 5-syllable word with primary stress on its 4th syllable. On the other hand, the word *father* is a 2-1 word, a 2-syllable word with primary stress on its 1st syllable. Such a simple numbering system provides a convenient shorthand for pinpointing syllable counts and primary word stress locations. Both teachers and students can use it to identify and remember the number of syllables in a word and its primary syllable stress. In language classrooms, I find that students pick up the two-digit system quickly (Murphy, 2004).

In addition to primary stress, longer words (e.g., words of four or more syllables) sometimes reveal a secondary stressed syllable. These are also stress locations, and they too feature the relatively clear enunciation of vowel sounds. However, secondary stresses tend not to be as loud or as prolonged as a word's primary stressed syllable. For example, while the primary stress in the 4-syllable word *economic* falls on its 3rd syllable, its 1st syllable also bears some secondary stress. When students are ready for this additional level of information, the numeric system can be expanded to include a third digit to signal a secondary stress. In this way, the word *economic* may be labeled as a 4-3-1 word (i.e., a 4-syllable word with primary stress on its 3rd syllable and secondary stress on its 1st syllable). Using the same conventions, the word *pronunciation* may be labeled 5-4-2 (5 syllables, primary stress on its 4th syllable, secondary stress on its 2nd syllable).

REFLECTIVE QUESTIONS

- Why might it be useful to use such a numeric system when teaching the pronunciation of individual words?

- How might you apply the system to words such as **eco_no_mic, metho_dol_ogy,** and *edu**ca**tion,* which have a secondary stressed syllable as well as a primary stressed syllable?

When learners return to the core language sample, they can begin to assign numeric labels for each of the sample's prominent words. Once established as a shared set of conventions, the labeling system is a useful tool for classroom discussion whenever questions about patterns of word stress arise. For easy reference, Murphy and Kandil (2004) provide a ranked ordering of the top 12 patterns of word stress in English:

Stress pattern	Illustration words	What the pattern means
3-2	commitment	3-syllable word, primary stress on 2nd syllable
2-2	approach	2-syllable word, primary stress on 2nd syllable
4-2	complexity	4-syllable word, primary stress on 2nd syllable
2-1	versions	2-syllable word, primary stress on 1st syllable
4-3-1	economic	4-syllable word, 3rd syllable carries primary stress, 1st syllable carries secondary stress
3-1	analyst	3-syllable word, 1st syllable carries primary stress,
4-1-3	qualitative	4-syllable word, 1st syllable carries primary stress, 3rd syllable carries secondary stress
3-1-3	institute	3-syllable word, 1st syllable carries primary stress, 3rd syllable carries secondary stress
5-3-1	methodologies	5-syllable word, 3rd syllable carries primary stress, 1st syllable carries secondary stress
5-2-4	discriminating	5-syllable word, 2nd syllable carries primary stress, 4th syllable carries secondary stress
4-2-4	facilitate	4-syllable word, 2nd syllable has primary stress 4th syllable has secondary stress
4-1	variable	4-syllable word, 1st syllable has primary stress

Conclusion

This chapter built upon the broader topics of chapters 1 through 3 by focusing on syllables and patterns of word stress of prominent words. In classrooms that follow the proposed instructional model, by this point students' oral rehearsals of core language samples will have included five essential features of English pronunciation: thought groups, prominence, featured words, syllable counts, and the location of primary stressed syllables. The chapter also introduced a handy numbering system intended to make it easier for students and teachers to discuss word stress patterns in class. The following Lesson Plan #2 illustrates one way of introducing the numbering system in an ESL/EFL classroom. In chapter 4, parallels were drawn between the operation of prominent words within thought groups and how primary stressed syllables operate within individual words. As a core component of pronunciation learning, any course featuring attention to vocabulary learning benefits from students having access to shared conventions for talking about syllable counts and patterns of word stress. Chapter 5 continues to build upon these themes by signaling intersections between word stress and the vowel system of English.

Lesson Plan #2
Syllable Counts and Word Stress

Level: Any	Time: 30–45 minutes
Sources: Murphy, J. (2004, 2014, 2017b); Murphy and Kandil (2004)	
Learning Objectives: Students will learn to use a simple numeric system for identifying the number of syllables in words and the location of primary stressed syllables. They will be able to apply the system to 10 to 15 words recently featured in their course materials.	
Language Foci: The number of syllables in the citation forms of words; patterns of word stress	
Anticipated Problems: Students may have a limited sense of syllable structure and patterns of word stress in spoken English. They may have difficulty identifying the number of syllables in words and/or the location of primary stressed syllables.	

continued on next page

Lesson Plan #2 *(continued)*

Solutions: Explain and define what syllables are. Show plenty of examples. Engage the class in a discussion of syllable counts for English words already known to them. Begin with easy, high-frequency words (e.g., *mother, machine, radio, solution, perhaps, introduce, experience, cigarette, necessary*), and then move on to words recently covered in course materials. Later, explain and define what constitutes a primary stressed syllable within a word. To engender motivation, explain the usefulness of shared classroom conventions for identifying and discussing syllable counts and the location of primary stressed syllables.

Materials: As illustrated in the Handout for Lesson Plan #2 that follows, create and distribute a handout illustrating a list of 10 to 20 English words that illustrate different numbers of syllables and different locations of primary stressed syllables. Also, create and distribute a skeleton version of the same handout that students will use as a template to enter words they self-select.

Classroom Procedures

1. Explain that knowing a word's number of syllables and the location of its primary stressed syllable are essential to knowing and being able to use the word in English.

2. Preview that the purpose of today's lesson is to learn easy classroom conventions for identifying and discussing syllable counts and primary stress locations of English words.

3. Solicit 10 or more words from students (e.g., easy words or words they have recently learned), and display these at the front of the room (e.g., *mother, machine, radio, solution, perhaps, introduce, experience, cigarette, necessary, pronunciation, photography, vocabulary*).

4. For each word displayed, ask students to identify its total number of syllables with a number (e.g., *mother* = 2, *machine* = 2, *radio* = 3, *solution* = 3, *perhaps* = 2, *introduce* = 3, *experience* = 4, *cigarette* = 3, *necessary* = 4, *pronunciation* = 5, *photography* = 4, *vocabulary* = 5).

5. Remind students that if they are unsure, some options are to check syllable counts with reference materials (e.g., the pronunciation key of a dictionary, an internet search), listen carefully as a proficient speaker pronounces the word, ask their teacher, or try to figure it out on their own.

6. Demonstrate to students that they can count syllables out on their fingers.

7. To reinforce this strategy, explain it is useful to develop a sensory feel for the number of syllables in a word by counting on their fingers, tapping on desktops, tapping their toes, or by using some other sort of physical gesture.

8. Label each word introduced with a single digit reflecting its total number of syllables (see step 4).

9. Then ask students which syllable is the strongest for each of the words they are examining (e.g., the 1st syllable of *mother*, the 2nd syllable of *machine*, the 1st syllable of *radio*, the 2nd syllable of *solution*, the 2nd syllable of *perhaps*, the 3rd syllable of *introduce*, the 4th syllable of *pronunciation*, the 2nd syllable of *photography*, the 2nd syllable of *vocabulary*).

continued on next page

Teaching Pronunciation

10. Refer to such a syllable as the word's primary stressed syllable, and explain that it is normally louder, has clearer vowel production, and takes a bit longer to say than any of the word's other syllables.

11. If students are unsure of primary stress locations, repeat steps 4 through 7 or encourage them to make educated guesses by applying rules for word stress (see, e.g., Celce-Murcia et al., 2010, pp. 187–194).

12. Especially with longer words, determine whether they have another strong-ish syllable (i.e., secondary stress). This optional step depends upon the proficiency level of the class.

13. As illustrated in the Handout for Lesson 2's last column, ask students to use a two-digit numeric system to label the syllable count (1st digit) and location of primary stress (2nd digit) for each word they examine. The introduction of this two-digit labeling system is the lesson's most important step. Some examples of the labeling system are: *mother* = 2-1 (i.e., a 2-syllable word with primary stress on its 1st syllable); *machine* 2-2 (a 2-syllable word with primary stress on its 2nd syllable; *radio* = 3-1 (a 3-syllable word with primary stress on its 1st syllable; *solution* = 3-2 (a 3-syllable word with primary stress on its 2nd syllable); *perhaps* = 2-2; *introduce* = 3-3; *experience* = 4-2.

14. Going forward in the course, especially whenever questions arise about the pronunciation of a word, begin any analysis or discussion by asking students to label the word under discussion with the two-digit numeric system. In this way, everyone in the classroom will share a basis for examining, learning, and remembering the pronunciation of words.

Caveats: For students at higher proficiency levels, the convention for keeping track of secondary stresses discussed in the chapter may also be introduced (e.g., *pronunciation* is 5-4-2 word; *economic* is a 4-3-1 word).

Beyond the classroom: As a recurring homework assignment, ask students to self-select and bring to class a list of 5 to 10 words that they have analyzed and labeled ahead of time according to the format featured in the Handout for Lesson Plan #2. At the start of a subsequent lesson, a few minutes may be dedicated to examining the syllable counts and primary stresses of students' self-selected vocabulary items. These procedures can be repeated as often as is relevant to students' needs and the nature of the course.

Handout for Lesson Plan #2
System for Identifying Syllable Counts and Primary Stress Locations

Illustration word	Number of syllables	Location of primary stressed syllable	Identification pattern
mother	2	1st syllable	2-1 (2-syllable word, primary stress on the 1st syllable)
machine	2	2nd syllable	2-2 (2-syllable word, primary stress on the 2nd syllable
radio	3	1st	3-1
solution	3	2nd	3-2
perhaps	2	2nd	2-2
introduce	3	3rd	3-3
experience	4	2nd	4-2
cigarette	3	3rd	3-3
necessary	4	1st	4-1
pronunciation	5	4th	5-4
photography	4	2nd	4-2
vocabulary	5	2nd	5-2
economic	4	3rd	4-3 (or 4-3-1 to signal secondary stress on 1st syllable)
majority	4	2nd	4-2
commitment	3	2nd	3-2
complexity	4	2nd	4-2
identification	6	5th	6-5 (or 6-5-2)

CHAPTER 5

The Vowel System

The topics addressed in this final chapter are intended to be featured in pronunciation-*centered* courses or courses in which pronunciation is given generous attention. Minimally, students will need to be aware of how thought groups, prominence, and primary stressed syllables contribute to the pronunciation of English to more fully appreciate how the vowel system of English operates.

Vowel Sounds

Learners of English need to know about vowel sounds because vowels serve as the acoustic peaks of primary stressed syllables (Murphy, 2017a; Rogerson-Revell, 2018). As such, vowels and the clear pronunciation of stressed syllables, prominent words, and thought groups are closely connected. When combined, these are the four elements that most contribute to the clarity of a speaker's pronunciation (Gilbert, 2009; Hahn, 2004). A premise of this final chapter is that if students are unfamiliar with the English vowel system, it also needs to be taught in class. However, for work with vowels to be productive, student awareness of thought groups, prominence, and primary stressed syllables needs to have been established first.

Just as prominent words serve as the peaks of individual thought groups and stressed syllables serve as the peaks of prominent words, vowel sounds serve as the peaks of primary stressed syllables. Collectively, these elements represent navigational guides listeners depend upon to understand a speaker's intended meaning (Gilbert, 2009). If we draw an analogy to the successive layers of an onion, vowels reside closest to the acoustic core of a spoken message, while the message's outer layers are the stressed syllables, prominent words, and thought groups enveloping them.

Chapters 1 through 4 recommended procedures for working with samples of spoken language that focus on thought grouping, prominence, and primary stressed syllables. Later, once attention shifts to the vowel system, teachers can guide students in working for a new purpose with language samples with which they are already familiar. Students' new task is to identify the vowel sounds that correspond with the primary stressed syllables of prominent words. For example, in the thought groups

// in b_ack of me // I heard a n_oi_se //

students would learn to recognize and then identify that the peak vowels of b_ack and n_oi_se rhyme with the vowels of h_at and b_oy, respectively. Clearly, teachers need to be available to support learners' efforts for productive work with vowel sounds to happen. Eventually, students' rehearsal tasks can begin to focus on their clearest enunciations possible of the peak vowels of prominent syllables. Here is some information about the system of English vowels teachers should be aware of:

1. Sixteen different vowel sounds feature in the pronunciation of most varieties of North American English.

2. English orthography has far fewer individual letters available to represent its 16 different vowel sounds. Along with other spelling conventions, different combinations of letters are commonly used to spell even a single vowel sound (e.g., d**ee**p, b**ea**ch, m**e**m**e**).

3. Due to the nature of English orthography, teachers should clearly differentiate between moments when they are working on either the pronunciation of English words (including the vowels contained within them) or the English system of either writing or spelling words. While some overlap exists between spoken and written English forms, these distinct systems of language reflect different sets of underlying conventions.

4. How the vowels of a word are pronounced varies considerably depending upon the role the word plays within a thought group (Cauldwell, 2018). For example, the stressed vowels of a prominent word within a thought group will be more clearly enunciated than the vowels of any neighboring nonprominent words (Murphy, 2017a). Similarly, the vowel of a prominent word's primary stressed syllable tends to be more clearly enunciated than other vowels within the same thought group or even within the same word (Cauldwell, 2013).

Table 5.1, following, presents all 16 vowels of North American English. It is intended to be used by both teachers and students in classrooms as a handy instructional tool. Copies of the table can serve as a handout for easy reference once students have gained some experience with its content. In Table 5.1, the vowels of English are numbered from 1 to 16. The pronunciation of each vowel is illustrated with five single-syllable words (with one exception). For example, the pronunciation of vowel sound #1 is illustrated with the words *deep*, *week*, *team*, *beach*, and *freeze*. For English speakers, all five of those words rhyme because each features the same vowel sound. In contrast, the pronunciation of vowel sound #12 is represented by the words *took*, *good*, *should*, *stood*, and *would*, all of which also rhyme in most versions of North American English.

Table 5.1. 16 English Vowels Matched with Single-Syllable Words

1) / iʸ /	2) / ɪ /	3) / eʸ /	4) / ɛ /
deep	hit	rain	said
week	tick	gate	bet
team	did	base	rest
beach	his	pain	ten
freeze	rich	play	get

5) / æ /	6) / ay /	7) / ɑ /	8) / aw /
pass	like	sock	pound
shack	lied	clock	town
grass	high	stop	now
back	life	hot	found
catch	my	got	out

9) / ɔ /	10) / ɔy /	11) / oʷ /	12) / ʊ /
ought	boy	float	took
thought	toy	slow	good
jaw	noise	vote	should
off	poise	close	stood
walk	joy	rope	wood

13) / uʷ /	14) / ə /[6]	15) / ʌ /	16) / ɜʳ /
soup	about	luck	bird
hoop	above	blood	heard
new	banana	cup	shirt
two	circus	mud	sir
who	America	tuck	dirt

From Murphy, J. [Ed.], Teaching the Pronunciation of English. Table 2.1 [p. 78]. Copyright © 2017, University of Michigan Press. Used with permission.

After distributing copies of Table 5.1 to the class, information-gap activities can be initiated in which students working in pairs prompt and quiz each other on the identification of vowel sounds (see Murphy 2003, 2017a). Although regional differences exist in how first language speakers of North American English pronounce several English vowels (Hazen, 2018), virtually all proficient speakers of English maintain enough similarity in their use of the vowel system to be able to understand each other with relative ease (Levis, 2018).

---

[6] Commonly referred to as the schwa, vowel 14 is best exemplified in multiple-syllable words because it appears only in unstressed positions in either a word or a thought group. Also, single-syllable function words such as a, the, and of normally use the same vowel.

Conclusion

This book promotes an innovative trajectory for teaching pronunciation in ESL/EFL classroom settings. Its starting point is the process of thought grouping (chapter 1), to which successive layers of the architecture of English pronunciation are then added in manageable increments. After the foundational role that thought groups play has been established, students begin to work through a sequence of several additional features of English pronunciation, each feature building upon those that came before. The proposed instructional sequence engages students in a process of working with prominence and featured words (chapter 3); syllables, patterns of word stress, and primary stressed syllables (chapter 4); as well as the system of English vowels (chapter 5). Beginning with thought groups and continuing throughout the entire sequence, students work in teams of two or small groups as they apply what they are learning to their collaborative analysis and rehearsals (aloud) of shared language samples. As discussed in chapter 2, teachers select language samples to best suit learners' needs. After students have worked through a full instructional sequence once, teachers introduce a new language sample, and the cycle repeats.

As learners gain more experience, teachers should explore both modifying and personalizing the ways of teaching pronunciation this book presents. When the time is right, a teacher might provide opportunities for students to self-select pronunciation features with which they would like to spend more time. Such decisions can be negotiated between teacher and students as one way of keeping learner motivation high. With teacher guidance and support, students can also begin to find and self-select language samples with which they would prefer to work. Finally, it is worth keeping in mind that when it comes to pronunciation learning, teachers can provide the most relevant information available, but ultimately learners' efforts are what really matter most. A crucial role for teachers is to encourage, guide, and support students' efforts.

References

Brazil, D. (1994). *Pronunciation for advanced learners of English*. New York, NY: Cambridge University Press.

Brown, H. D., & Lee, H. (2015). *Teaching by principles: An Interactive approach to language pedagogy* (4th ed.). Englewood Cliffs, NJ: Prentice-Hall.

Brown, G. (1977). *Listening to spoken English*. London, England: Routledge.

Cauldwell, R. (2002). The functional irrhythmicality of spontaneous speech: A discourse view of speech rhythms. *Apples: Journal of Applied Language Studies, 2*, 1–24.

Cauldwell, R. (2013). *Phonology for listening: Teaching the stream of speech*. Birmingham, England: Speech in Action.

Cauldwell, R. (2018). *A syllabus for listening: Decoding*. Birmingham, England: Speech in Action.

Celce-Murcia, M., Brinton, D., Goodwin, J., & Griner, B. (2010). *Teaching pronunciation: A course book and reference guide* (2nd ed.). New York, NY: Cambridge University Press.

Cutler, A. (2015). Lexical stress in English pronunciation. In M. Reed & J. Levis (Eds.), *The handbook of English pronunciation* (pp. 106–124). Oxford, England: Wiley Blackwell.

Dauer, R. (1993). *Accurate English: A complete course in pronunciation*. Englewood Cliffs, NJ: Regents Prentice Hall.

Derwing, T. M., & Munro, M. J. (2015). *Pronunciation fundamentals: Evidence-based perspectives for L2 teaching and research*. Philadelphia. PA: John Benjamins.

Dickerson, W. (2010). Walking the walk: Integrating the story of English phonology. In J. M. Levis & K. LeVelle (Eds.), *Proceedings of the 1st pronunciation in second language learning and teaching conference* (pp. 10–23). Ames, IA: Iowa State University.

Fanselow, J. (1987). *Breaking rules.* New York, NY: Longman.

Field, J. (2005). Intelligibility and the listener: The role of lexical stress. *TESOL Quarterly, 39,* 399–423.

Field, J. (2008). Listening in the language classroom. Cambridge, England: Cambridge University Press.

Gilbert, J. (2009). *Teaching pronunciation using the prosody pyramid.* New York, NY: Cambridge University Press.

Goodwin, J. (2001). Teaching pronunciation. In M. Celce-Murcia, D. M. Brinton, & M. A. Snow (Eds.), *Teaching English as a second or foreign language* (3rd ed., pp. 117–137). Boston, MA: Heinle Cengage.

Grant, L. (2007). *Well said intro: Pronunciation for clear communication.* Boston, MA: Thomson/Heinle & Heinle.

Grant, L. (2017). *Well said: Pronunciation for clear communication* (4th ed.). Boston, MA: National Geographic/Cengage Learning.

Hahn, L. (2004). Primary stress and intelligibility: Research to motivate the teaching of suprasegmentals. *TESOL Quarterly, 38,* 201–223.

Han, F. (2016). Integrating pronunciation instruction with passage-level reading instruction. In T. Jones (Ed.), *Integrating pronunciation with other skills areas* (pp. 143–151). Alexandria, VA: TESOL International Association.

Hazen, K. (2018). Standards of pronunciation and regional English. In O. Kang, R. Thomson, & J. Murphy (Eds.), *The Routledge handbook of contemporary English pronunciation* (pp. 189–202). London and New York: Routledge.

Jones, T. (Ed.). (2016). *Integrating pronunciation with other skills areas.* Alexandria, VA: TESOL.

Lane, L. (2010). *Tips for teaching pronunciation: A practical approach.* White Plains, NY: Pearson/Longman.

Levis, J. (1999). Intonation in theory and practice, revisited. *TESOL Quarterly, 33,* 37–63.

Levis, J. (2018). *Intelligibility, oral communication, and the teaching of pronunciation.* Cambridge, England: Cambridge University Press.

Miller, S., & Jones, T. (2016). Taking the fear factor out of integrating pronunciation and beginning grammar. In T. Jones (Ed.), *Integrating pronunciation with other skills areas* (pp. 89–101). Alexandria, VA: TESOL.

Morley, J. (1994). A multidimensional curriculum design for speech-pronunciation interaction. In J. Morley (Ed.), *Pronunciation pedagogy and theory: New views, new directions* (pp. 64–91). Alexandria, VA: TESOL.

Murphy, J. M. (2003). *Pronunciation.* In D. Nunan (Ed.), *Practical English language teaching* (pp. 111–128). New York, NY: McGraw-Hill.

Murphy, J. M. (2004). Attending to word-stress while learning new vocabulary. *English for Specific Purposes, 23*, 67–83.

Murphy, J. M. (2014). Learning word stress along with new vocabulary. In A. Coxhead (Ed.), *New Ways in Teaching Vocabulary, Revised* (pp. 21–24). Alexandria, VA: TESOL.

Murphy, J. (2015). Clearer speech through the process of thought grouping. In M. Lewis & H. Reinders (Eds.), *New ways in teaching adults* (pp. 121–123). Alexandria, VA: TESOL.

Murphy, J. M. (2016). Pronunciation, thought grouping, & general listening skills. In T. Jones (Ed.), *Integrating pronunciation with other skills areas* (pp. 57–74). Alexandria, VA: TESOL.

Murphy, J. M. (2017a). Segmentals: Phonemes, allophones, vowel sounds, consonants, and squeeze zones. In J. Murphy (Ed.), *Teaching the Pronunciation of English: Focus on Whole Courses* (pp. 70–106). Ann Arbor, MI: University of Michigan Press.

Murphy, J. M. (2017b). Suprasegmentals: Thought groups, prominence, word stress, intonation, and pitch jumps. In J. Murphy (Ed.), *Teaching the Pronunciation of English: Focus on Whole Courses* (pp. 31–69). Ann Arbor, MI: University of Michigan Press.

Murphy, J. M. (2017c). Teacher training in the teaching of pronunciation. In O. Kang, R. Thomson & J. Murphy (Eds). *The Routledge handbook of second language pronunciation* (pp. 298–319). London and New York: Routledge.

Murphy, J. M., & Kandil, M. (2004). Word-level stress patterns in the academic word list. *System, 32*(1), 61–74.

Reed, M. (2016). Listening to what is meant: Illocution. In T. Jones (Ed.) *Pronunciation in the classroom* (pp. 75–87). Alexandria, VA: TESOL.

Rimmer, W. (2016). Integrating pronunciation with advanced grammar. In T. Jones (Ed.). *Pronunciation in the classroom* (pp. 115–127). Alexandria, VA: TESOL.

Rogerson-Revell, P. (2018). English vowels and consonants. In O. Kang, R. Thomson, & J. Murphy (Eds.), *The Routledge handbook of contemporary English pronunciation* (pp. 93–121). London and New York: Routledge.

Sardegna, V., Chiang, F., & Ghosh, M. (2016). Integrating pronunciation with presentation skills. In T. Jones (Ed.), *Pronunciation in the classroom* (pp. 43–55). Alexandria, VA: TESOL.

Wong, R. (1987). *Teaching pronunciation: Focus on English rhythm and intonation.* Englewood Cliffs, NJ: Regents Prentice Hall.

Appendix

Answer Key for the Airplane Aisle Incident Activity

For more advanced work (1) draw a circle around any featured words within each thought group; and (2) underline the most prominent single word within each thought group. The first three items have been completed for you (featured words in bold print; prominent words are also underlined).

Thought Groups (featured words indicated in bold)	Likely Number of Featured Words
// the plane **land**ed //	1 (*landed* is prominent)
// the **cabin** lights turned on //	2 (*cabin* is prominent; *on* is featured)
// **every**one got out of their seats //	2 (though either *everyone* or *seats* could be made prominent)[7]

continued on next page

---

[7] Variation is possible because the system of prominence is flexible and depends on the speaker's communicative intent.

(Continued)

Thought Groups (featured words indicated in bold)	Likely Number of Featured Words
// I stepped into the aisle //	2
// opened the overhead compartment //	2 (possibly 3)
// and was waiting my turn to leave the plane //	3 (possibly 2)
// in back of me //	1
// I heard a **noise** that **didn't** sound **right** //	3 (possibly 4)
// when I **turned** //	1
// I saw an **older** man //	1 (possibly 2)
// was **falling** into a woman **behind** him //	2 (possibly 3)
// he looked **scared** //	1
// his **face** was **stone white** //	3 (possibly 2)
// I didn't think he was **breathing** //	2
// I **yelled** for **help** //	2
// and then a **couple** of us moved into **action** //	2 (possibly 3)
// the **first** thing I did //	1
// was to get the people **behind** me to back **away** //	2 (possibly 3)
// by **this** point most of the **aisle** had **cleared** //	3
// so we were able to **stretch** him out on the **floor** //	2
// I **heard** someone **say** //	2 (possibly 1)
// we **have** to get him **out** of the plane //	2 (possibly 3)
// so I **grabbed** his **legs** //	2 (possibly 1)
// this **tall** guy grabbed his **shoulders** //	2 (possibly 3)
// and we **carried** him **off** //	2 (possibly 1)

continued on next page

Teaching Pronunciation

(Continued)

Thought Groups (featured words indicated in bold)	Likely Number of Featured Words
// I know **CPR** //	4 (if it's // C // P // R //)
// so I **cleared** a space //	1 (possibly 2)
// made sure **everyone** else was **out** of the **way** //	3 (possibly 4)
// fortunately //	1 (which syllable?)
// when it was all **over** //	1 (possibly 2)
// he fully **recovered** //	1 (possibly 2)
// **seemed** to be **fine** //	2 (possibly 1)